Vintage

Cocktails

Vintage

Cocktails

*Authentic Recipes and Illustrations
from 1920-1960*

SUSAN WAGGONER AND ROBERT MARKEL

SMITHMARK

Project Director: Elizabeth Viscott Sullivan
Editor: Tricia Levi
Designer: Kay Schuckhart/Blond on Pond
Printed in Singapore
10 9 8 7 6 5 4 3 2 1

This edition published in 1999 by SMITHMARK Publishers,
a division of U.S. Media Holdings, Inc.,
115 West 18th Street, New York, NY, 10011.

SMITHMARK books are available for bulk purchase for sales
promotion and premium use. For details write or call the manager
of special sales, SMITHMARK Publishers, 115 West 18th Street,
New York, NY 10011; 212-519-1215.

Library of Congress Cataloging-in-Publication Data
Waggoner, Susan.
    Vintage cocktails : authentic recipes and illustrations from
1920-1960 / Susan Waggoner and Robert Markel.
        p. cm.
    Includes bibliographical references and index.
    ISBN: 0-7651-1733-9 (hc.)
    1. Cocktails.   I. Markel, Robert.
TX951.W26   1999
641.8'74—dc21   99-27322
                                        CIP

Contents

History

It's cocktail time. Few phrases flood the senses with such unimpeded tingles of delight. The mind rushes to imagine the astringent whiff of gin, the ice-cold silver shaker, the first pleasant trickle accompanied by the certainty that the world will soon seem a much better place than it appeared to be just a few minutes ago.

Like Marilyn Monroe, the cocktail has become one of the great cultural icons of the twentieth century. Yet, however modern it may seem, the cocktail's actual origins date back much further. The drink is at least a nineteenth-century invention and, in all probability, a gift from the eighteenth century. In fact, the cocktail's lifeline stretches so far back that the origin of the word itself can no longer be determined with certainty. There are many competing stories, as is almost always the case with ingenious inventions.

Several stories assert that the word is a pairing of the words "cock" and "ale" or "tail." One version insists that it's named after the fortified ale given to fighting cocks before a contest. Another insists that Betsy Flannigan, a Pennsylvania innkeeper, used cock tail feathers as swizzle sticks when serving drinks during the American Revolution. A less romantic story pairs the cock, or spigot, of a whiskey keg with the "tail" end leavings in the keg—dregs so bitter that they needed the addition of other ingredients to be palatable. A somewhat later account betrays an early impulse to give the cocktail more elegant origins. According to this story, New Orleans apothecary Antoine Peychaud mixed drinks in a French egg cup,

> Let there be dancing in the streets, drinking in the saloons, and necking in the parlor.
>
> ~ Groucho Marx as Otis B. Driftwood in A NIGHT AT THE OPERA, 1935

7

IN A GLASS

or coquetier. Over the years, the word was transformed into the nearest English equivalent, "cocktail." Whatever its origins, the word first appeared in print in 1806 in *The Balance*, an early American magazine that defined it as a drink "composed of spirits of any kind, sugar, water, and bitters."

Throughout the nineteenth century, the cocktail remained a rough-and-tumble product, drunk almost exclusively by men—and usually not men of the better sort. We can see just how out of place cocktails were in better circles from the menus of the doomed Titanic, which list a dazzling variety of wines, champagnes, sherries, and ports without a single mention of before-dinner or after-dinner mixed drinks.

The first efforts to incorporate cocktails into high society were somewhat tepid. American hotels, which had followed the British tradition of five o'clock tea, began

offering mixed drinks as late-afternoon refreshment. To preserve the air of acceptable gentility, early shakers were even made in the shape of teapots, and the magic hour was called "tea time" long after tea vanished from the scene.

All this changed a very few years later, when modernism, World War I, and flaming youth reshaped the world. The generation that fought the Great War found itself in need of a bracer—and not only men, but women, began to drink cocktails with impunity. The Old Order responded to this outrage by imposing Prohibition, but the effort fostered more drinking and spawned

more cocktails than years of legality ever had. With the repeal of Prohibition, Americans again took up the shaker, flask, and glass and held on tight through another world war and the effervescent boom of the 1950s. Today, a whole new generation is discovering the cocktail's sublime elegance—a cultural undertaking we raise our glasses to in hearty salute. Here's looking at you, kids.

Here's How: 5 Basic Techniques

Cocktails are not difficult to make, provided one knows a few basic techniques. Master these, add a generous dash of élan, and you'll soon be the envy of smart sets everywhere you go.

FLOAT To float one liquid atop another, heavier one, insert a bar spoon or large spoon into the glass, rounded side up, just above the surface of the liquid. Pour the liquid you wish to float slowly over the back of the spoon.

MUDDLE A muddler is a very small pestle, usually made of wood but also of glass or plastic. It is used to crush, or muddle, ingredients together in the bottom of the glass before adding other ingredients. In the grand old days, muddlers were served with the drink, as swizzle sticks are today. There is really no efficient replacement for a proper muddler, and purchasing one is a worthwhile investment.

SHAKE The chief failing of amateurs is to give too brief a shake—an error, since drinks are generally shaken because they contain ingredients that do not combine easily and need brisk assistance. Another error is to hold the shaker upright, with one's hand around the middle. The correct way is to hold the shaker horizontally with a hand at either end, a position that reduces the amount of body heat transferred to the shaker. We prefer the classic silver metal shaker, since it keeps drinks colder than a glass one does. However, should you happen to find yourself stranded on a desert island, any jar with a lid will do.

STIR   Drinks such as highballs made with spirits and soda or water, whose ingredients combine easily, require no more than a very brief stir to finish. Use a long-handled bar spoon or swizzle stick.

STRAIN   If you have stirred a drink in a mixing glass or shaken it in a shaker, it is imperative to strain the drink into a serving glass. This is true even if the drink is to be served with ice, in which case you should place new ice in the serving glass and discard the old ice. The reason for this is that the old ice has already begun to melt because of the friction of stirring and shaking. New ice will keep the drink colder. If you have a proper bar strainer, so much the better. However, the lid of the shaker can also be used effectively.

Tips for a Perfect Cocktail

Here are some additional secrets, the result of exhaustive hours of research and observation.

1. Chilled glasses are a must. Place them in the freezer an hour before use, or flash-chill by filling with crushed ice 15 minutes ahead of time.

2. Make sure that soda, fruit juices, and other mixers are thoroughly chilled.

3. Make drinks in batches, rather than one at a time. Individually made drinks become warm more quickly.

4. Use footed cocktail glasses when appropriate, and handle all glasses from the base. This minimizes the transference of body heat to the glass.

5. Once made, a cocktail must be served immediately. If not, it will begin to separate. (This is why Pousse Cafés may be made ahead of time.)

6. Never refill a glass. Use a clean, fresh, well-chilled glass for each drink—even if your guests are far past noticing.

Vintage Cocktails

Americano

Italians had been trying to sell Americans on the taste of Campari for decades when, more than seventy years after the bitters' 1861 debut, a modified cocktail finally caught on. Yankee expats, fleeing Prohibition, made their way to Italy—and discovered the one drink that could be taken back to the U.S. and legally imbibed there. Classified as a medicinal product rather than a spirit, Campari escaped the lethal ax of the law. Impressed by the Yanks' appreciation of their national treasure, Italians dubbed the drink "The Americano."

Original recipes for this drink called for a 2:1 ratio of Campari to sweet vermouth, but over time the dominance of Campari waned. Later recipes evened the ratio, and modern recipes often describe an Americano—illegitimately—as a vermouth drink with a "dash" of bitters.

> **A HUNDRED YEARS FROM NOW—WHAT?**
> The beverage use of alcohol will be utterly unknown except among the abnormal, subnormal, vicious, and depraved, which classes will largely have been bred out of the race in America.
>
>
>
> ~William Anderson,
> Anti-Saloon League of N.Y.,
> asked to forecast the future,
> THE WORLD, 1923

Americano

1 oz. Campari

$^1/_2$ oz. sweet vermouth (1 oz., if you must)

Club soda

Orange wheel garnish

In a highball glass, stir Campari and sweet vermouth together with ice cubes. Add club soda and garnish with orange.

FOR YOUR FURTHER DRINKING PLEASURE: If an Americano doesn't quite deliver the jolt you're looking for, the following is a bracing variation. Prohibition is over, after all, so there's no harm in trying a Negroni, the invention of Count Camillo Negroni, who ordered his Americanos with gin instead of club soda. To make a proper Negroni, increase Campari and sweet vermouth to $1^1/_2$ oz. each, add $1^1/_2$ oz. gin, and stir. The orange wheel is, as before, a welcome garnish.

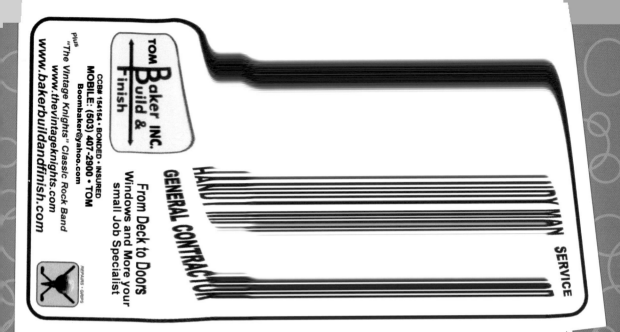
This creamy concoction was one of Prohibition's most popular after-dinner drinks, imbibed by sweet young things from New York to Rio. When made correctly and punctuated with a well-placed garnish, the *raison d'être* of its slightly naughty name becomes angelically clear. Some recipes call for equal parts maraschino and cream, with the cream whipped to a stiff froth. We prefer this version which is simpler to make and a joy to drink.

1$\frac{1}{2}$ oz. maraschino liqueur

$\frac{3}{4}$ oz. fresh cream

Maraschino cherry garnish

Pour maraschino liqueur into a cocktail glass, float cream on top, and garnish with a perfectly centered cherry.

FOR YOUR FURTHER DRINKING PLEASURE: Almost as old as the Angel's Tit is its less risqué cousin, the Angel's Tip. Follow the same recipe and method, using crème de cacao instead of maraschino liqueur and withholding the cherry.

Aviation

Should you be so lucky as to have a bottle of maraschino liqueur on hand, don't pass up a chance to try this delectable 1930s gin drink. Like the name, the taste conjures visions of air races, velocity, and sleek, light-winged craft.

> MARASCHINO:
> delicious cherry derivative,
> fermented and distilled, then flavored by the
> bruised cherry stones themselves. Maraschino is so essential that
> no fairly equipped bar can afford to be without it.
>
> ~Charles Baker, THE GENTLEMAN'S COMPANION, 1939

1½ oz. gin

Juice of 1 lemon, strained of seeds

1 tbsp. maraschino liqueur

In a cocktail shaker, pour gin, lemon juice, and maraschino over cracked ice. Shake vigorously and strain into a cocktail glass. This drink is all the better if the glass is chilled; if not, allow a few small slivers of ice to slip through the strainer.

DANZÓN CUBANA

SIBONEY

(SEE-BO-NAY)

A QUAINT &
ORIGINAL MELODY
ALL HAVANA
DANCES TO

by
ERNESTO
LECUO
American Lyr
by DoLL
MOR

POPULAR EDITION

Bacardi Cocktail

If you fail to make this classic with genuine Bacardi rum, somebody turn out the lights and call the law—you've just violated a statute. In 1936, Bacardi became so irked with bars' propensity for using no-name rum in this cocktail that the company took the matter to court. Bacardi won, the defendants appealed, and the state of New York upheld in the company's favor. Thus was the authentic Bacardi cocktail preserved for future generations.

1¹/₂ oz. Bacardi rum

Juice of 1 lime, strained of seeds

1 tsp. grenadine

Maraschino cherry garnish

Place rum, lime juice, and grenadine in a cocktail shaker with cracked ice. Shake rapidly and strain into a cocktail glass. Thread the cherry on a toothpick or cocktail sword and lay across the rim of the glass.

FOR YOUR FURTHER DRINKING PLEASURE: In the classic guide to drinking, THE GENTLEMAN'S COMPANION, Charles Baker describes the Bertita, "an Exotic We Have Personally Fetched Back from Taxco . . . where Artists from America Congregate for Varying Reasons, & with Varying Success." To make the drink, double the quantity of rum, add the juice of half an orange, combine with lime juice and grenadine, and shake with finely cracked ice. Serve unstrained in a champagne flute, omitting the garnish.

～1936～

In addition to the landmark Bacardi ruling, here are some other headlines from the year.

GONE WITH THE WIND shatters publishing records.

Jesse Owens infuriates Der Führer by winning four gold medals at the Berlin Olympics.

Edward VIII abdicates in favor of his true vocation, Wallis Simpson.

The minimum wage for women is ruled unconstitutional.

Shirley Temple wonders aloud, "Suppose I'm not so cute when I grow up as I am now?"

Unemployment hovers at 16.9%. Luckily, the price of aspirin is held to a modest 15¢ a dozen.

Between the Sheets

This after-Prohibition after-dinner drink was meant to seduce as well as settle. It accomplishes both. While most recipes call for ordinary brandy, this elegant version—made at the bar of Jerusalem's King David Hotel in the 1930s—is preferred.

> Prohibition has taken away the incentive for leisure at the table.
>
>
>
> ~James R. McCarthy, in PEACOCK ALLEY, A HISTORY OF THE WALDORF, 1931

1 oz. cognac

1 oz. Cointreau

1 oz. dry gin

Juice of 2 lemons, strained of seeds

Put plenty of cracked ice in a cocktail shaker, add ingredients, and shake briskly. Strain into a cocktail glass. To make a drier drink, reduce the amount of Cointreau.

Bloody Mary

The drink that almost everyone knows today has a past that few know and even fewer agree upon. The undisputed fact is that a prototype of the drink was mixed by the famous bartender Fernand "Pete" Petiot at Harry's Bar in Paris, circa 1921, and dubbed a "Bucket of Blood" by one of the bar's patrons. After Prohibition's repeal, Petiot took a position at the St. Regis Hotel's King Cole Bar in New York, bringing his armamentarium of drinks with him. However, the swank St. Regis feared the Bloody Mary's gruesome name might offend some patrons, so the drink made its stateside debut as the Red Snapper.

The Bloody Mary is a relatively recent addition to the cocktail roster. The classic drink books of the 1920s and 1930s—including *The Bon Vivant's Companion* by drink "Professor" Jerry Thomas, Patrick Gavin Duffy's *The Official Drink Mixer's Manual*, and Charles Baker's *The Gentleman's Companion*—don't mention it. Indeed, very few vodka drinks appear in bartender's guides written before World War II. Gin was the "clear" of the moment, getting a boost from the scarcity of vodka and, ironically, from Prohibition. As Americans quickly discovered during the Great Experiment, gin is one of the easier liquors to fabricate, and the tides of bathtub gin imbibed from 1920 to 1933, when the Volstead Act was in force, created a craving for gin drinks that would last a generation.

SMIRNOFF'S LUCKY CORKS

Smirnoff's eventual domination of the American vodka market began
with a lucky fluke. The brand's first U.S. distillery started production in the
mid-1930s, but Americans' preference for gin made for tough competition. The
company nevertheless produced so many cases of the stuff that the production
line ran out of corks and had to use corks labeled "Smirnoff's Whiskey."
Quick-thinking salesmen began promoting the brew as a variety of whiskey—
colorless, odorless, and tasteless. This concept proved far more beguiling than the
idea of vodka had ever been, and sales took a major leap forward.

Bloody Mary

3 oz. tomato juice

Juice of $\frac{1}{2}$ lemon, strained of seeds

$1\frac{1}{2}$ oz. vodka

1–2 dashes Worcestershire Sauce

Black pepper to taste

Pour tomato and lemon juices over ice in a highball glass. Add vodka and spices
and stir. Note that the original Bloody Mary was served with a conventional
swizzle stick, not the celery stalk that became popular from the 1960s onward.
The original Bloody Mary also lacked Tabasco, which is now a common ingredient.
Other modern spicings include celery salt and horseradish.

FOR YOUR FURTHER DRINKING PLEASURE: Whatever its
disputed past, the gin Red Snapper deserves to be revived. Follow the recipe
and directions above, replacing vodka with the same amount of gin.

Caipirinha

The original Brazilian bombshell, the caipirinha (pronounced kigh-puh-reen-yah) is made of sugar, lime, and cachaça (kah-shah-sah), a high-proof product distilled from sugarcane. An invention not of bars or bartenders, the caipirinha is a workingman's tradition that dates well back in time. When American companies in search of tin, rubber, and other commodities expanded operations to the southern continent it was an ingrained habit. The abstemious Henry Ford tried to wean workers off the drink, but the tide of history—and taste—was against him. The caipirinha's popularity was too entrenched to overcome. To make matters even worse from Mr. Ford's point of view, Americans in flight from the rigors of Prohibition stumbled upon the drink and took the recipe home with them.

> PROHIBITION REPEAL IS RATIFIED AT 5:32 PM ROOSEVELT ASKS NATION TO BAR THE SALOON NEW YORK CELEBRATES WITH QUIET RESTRAINT—
> City Toasts New Era
> Crowds Swamp the Legal Resorts
> But Legal Liquor is Still Rare
>
>
>
> ~NEW YORK TIMES headline, December 5, 1933

Caipirinha

1 small lime

1 1/2 tsp. sugar

1 1/2 oz. cachaça

Cut the top and bottom off the lime, then cut lengthwise in quarters and place in an old-fashioned glass, skin side down. Add sugar and, using a pestle, crush lime and muddle until sugar is dissolved. Fill the glass nearly to the top with crushed ice, pour in the cachaça, and stir. Note: If you do not have cachaça on hand, high-proof rum will give you a fair but not quite authentic approximation of the drink.

FOR YOUR FURTHER DRINKING PLEASURE: The Caipirinha is a close relative and probable forerunner of the Crusta. According to THE BON VIVANT'S COMPANION, published in the 1920s, the Crusta was invented by Santina, a Spanish caterer. To make this drink, pare a lemon or lime in a spiral strip. Dip the spiral of citrus rind in the juice of its fruit, then into sugar. Place this in a glass, and add juice, ice, and alcohol. While most Crusta recipes call for rum, we have also seen brandy, whiskey, and gin variations.

Champagne Cocktails

The taste for champagne cocktails may have originated in Victorian London when, in 1861, the Empire was mourning Prince Albert. To keep pace with the somber national mood, the head barman at the Brooks' Club combined pale champagne with an equal amount of chilled dark Guinness and dubbed the resulting drink a

Black Velvet (also known as a Champagne Velvet). By the twentieth century, champagne cocktails were a sophisticated staple at bars around the world. Lest you think champagne a bit dainty, remember that it's the drink of choice in *Casablanca*—what Humphrey Bogart is quaffing when he says, "Here's looking at you, kid."

Classic I

Sipped in New York even before the turn of the century, this may have been the first cocktail deemed appropriate for women of society—many of whose daughters would soon become flappers and literally bathe in the stuff.

1 sugar cube

Angostura bitters

Champagne

Saturate the sugar cube with bitters and place in a chilled flute. Fill to the brim with the best champagne you can afford.

MARGO: Encore du champagne.
WAITER: More champagne, Miss
Channing?
MARGO: That's what I said, bub.

We don't hold you up here

~Bette Davis in ALL ABOUT EVE, 1950

Classic II

Referred to as a Maharajah's Burra Peg by Charles Baker in *The Gentleman's Companion* and called a Business Brace by the bartender who invented it in 1889, this variation is often given as the "classic" champagne cocktail. Although the above recipe, featured in both *The Bon Vivant's Companion* and *The Official Mixer's Manual*, is the true classic, it's not worth quibbling about—this drink is far too good to take issue with.

1 sugar cube

Angostura bitters

$1\frac{1}{2}$ oz. cognac

Champagne

Saturate the sugar cube with bitters and place in a chilled flute. Add cognac, then fill the glass to the top with champagne. If you desire a garnish, a spiral of lime peel will do very nicely.

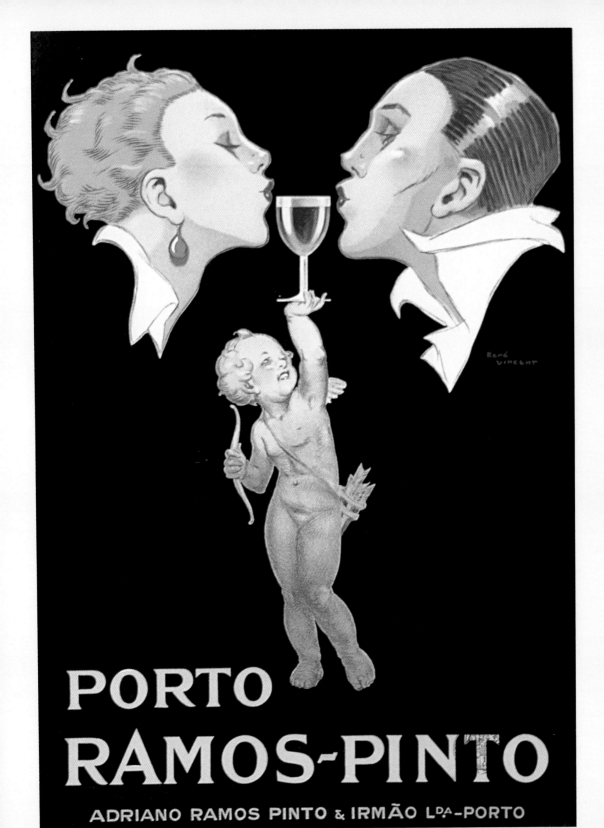

PORTO
RAMOS-PINTO
ADRIANO RAMOS PINTO & IRMÃO Lᴅᴬ-PORTO

Bellini

The warm, delicate glow of Bellini's paintings aroused such admiration in Giuseppe Cipriani, bartender at Harry's Bar in Venice in the 1940s, that he decided to concoct a drink of the same entrancing hue.

1 1/2 oz. fresh peach
juice
Champagne

STERNWOOD: How do you like your brandy, sir?
MARLOWE: In a glass.
STERNWOOD: I used to like mine with champagne. Champagne cold as Valley Forge and with about three ponies of brandy under it.... I like to see people drink.

~Charles Waldron and Humphrey Bogart in THE BIG SLEEP, 1946

The time and effort involved in using fresh juice in this recipe will be well rewarded. To do so, peel and puree several fresh peaches. Strain by placing the pulp in cheesecloth and twisting. Place juice in a chilled flute and fill with dry champagne. To enjoy this drink in the winter, we advise freezing an ample supply of peach pulp during the summer months.

30

Kir Royale

Next time you're challenged to say something good about the French, offer this in their defense: they invented the Kir Royale. Originally a combination of cassis and wine enjoyed by the farm and vineyard workers of Burgundy, this drink was first known merely as Kir, named after a popular local mayor and war hero. When champagne replaced the Burgundy wine, the drink acquired its royal status.

1/2 oz. cassis
Champagne

Pour the cassis in a chilled flute and add champagne.

Mimosa

The idea of blending champagne with orange goes back to the classic cocktail, when adventurous drinkers soaked sugar cubes in orange bitters rather than in Angostura. The combination reached its peak at the Ritz Hotel in Paris, where this drink was popular from the mid-1920s on. When making this drink, please resist the fad for turning it into a bland soda-pop-like brunch drink. In a proper mimosa, the kick of champagne dominates, and the

CONTRA

dash of Grand Marnier builds complexity.

Fresh orange juice
Generous dash of Grand Marnier
Champagne

Fill a well-chilled flute no more than 1/3 full with fresh orange juice. Add Grand Marnier, then fill with champagne.

The Collins Clan

We owe this, one of the oldest of the classic cocktails, to John Collins, barman at Limmer's Hotel in London. In the early 1800s, Collins invented a drink composed of dry Dutch gin, sugar, lemon, and soda water. Experimenters soon expanded on his idea, replacing the Dutch gin with a sweeter variety known as Old Tom. To distinguish between the two versions, the newcomer was dubbed a Tom Collins. It quickly proved more popular than the original John Collins, and its fame spread throughout the Empire. The drink gained a foothold in the U.S. when World War I veterans brought it back here from over there, and has been extremely popular ever since.

While the original Collins is composed of gin, sugar, lemon juice, and soda, the recipe is an irresistible invitation to experiment, and its ingredients go well with a variety of liquors. As a result, we have an entire Collins family to choose from, and it's worthwhile to know each of these tasty clan members by name.

Give me a bromide. And put some gin in it.

~Mary Boland in
THE WOMEN, 1939

1 tsp. sugar

Juice of 1 lemon, strained of seeds

$1\frac{1}{2}$ oz. gin

Club soda

Place three or more ice cubes in a tall glass. Add sugar and lemon juice. Pour in gin, then fill to the top with club soda and stir. The now-ubiquitous cherry garnish is a thoroughly modern invention and, from our point of view, gratuitous.

To make these members of the Collins clan, follow the recipe above, replacing gin with the liquor specified.

BRANDY COLLINS: brandy

JACK COLLINS: applejack

SANDY COLLINS: scotch

PEDRO COLLINS: rum

BACARDI COLLINS: Bacardi rum

MIKE COLLINS: Irish whiskey

JOHN COLLINS: bourbon

33

FOR YOUR FURTHER DRINKING PLEASURE: There are so many offspring of the original Collinses that one could easily devote a book to them. One of the stars of the family is the Mojito. As perfected at Sloppy Joe's in Havana, the Mojito calls for good light rum and the juice of a lime rather than a lemon. But the true secret of the Mojito's lovely fresh-bitter taste lies in adding lime peel to the drink and garnishing it with a generous sprig of mint whose leaves have been slightly crushed. A similar drink, called a Gin Buck, is a Mojito made with ginger ale rather than club soda and served without the mint garnish.

Cuba Libre

According to court documents filed many years after the fact, the first Cuba Libre was mixed in Cuba in August 1900. But as detectives often point out, time clouds evidence, and we're willing to bet that the practice of mixing rum with Coca-Cola is at least a few years older than its birth certificate. While some experts assert that it didn't become popular until after World War II, our favorite intrepid imbiber Charles Baker reports that by the late 1920s it was ubiquitous from Palm Beach to Seattle. We agree with Baker's lament that, all too often, the Cuba Libre is indistinguishable from rum and Coke. We therefore offer his recipe for an "analyzed and improved" version of the drink, which cuts the sweetness with the refreshing bite of lime peel.

1 small lime

$1^1/_2$ oz. Bacardi rum

Coca-Cola

Cut lime and strain juice into a tall Collins glass. Scrape peel clean, cut in pieces, and add peel to the glass. Pour in rum. Muddle, working so that the sides of the glass are coated with liquid. Then add ice and Coca-Cola.

The Daiquiri

In an oft-repeated version of the Daiquiri's origin, the time is 1898 and the place is the miasmatic, malarial swampland of Cuba. With mosquitoes in abundance and antimalarial medication yet to be invented, it's said that rum was added to drinking water as a fever preventative. Subsequent tinkering to make the remedy more palatable eventually produced this now-famous drink. Named for the small town of Daiquirí, near Santiago on the west coast of Cuba, the drink's true origin may be more mundane. Jennings Cox, an American mining engineer working in Cuba, is said to have invented the drink one night when, with company expected at any moment, he ran out of gin. These tales overlook the probability that the real forerunner of the Daiquiri was invented by native Cubans, who had ready access to the basic ingredients of rum, lime juice, and sugar.

However it came into being, the daiquiri's fame spread rapidly. Imported to America by Navy Admiral Lucas Johnson in 1909, it became so popular at Washington's Army and Navy Club that

> SARAH: These are delicious . . . What's in it?
> SKY: Oh, sugar and a sort of native flavoring
> SARAH: What's the name of the flavoring?
> SKY: Bacardi
>
> ~Sky Masterson and Sarah Brown visit Havana in
> GUYS AND DOLLS, 1950

a brass plaque in the club's Daiquiri Lounge now honors Cox's name. Characters in F. Scott Fitzgerald's *This Side of Paradise* (1920) order Daiquiris with the nonchalance of long-standing familiarity, and by the 1930s, it was possible to order this superb drink almost anywhere on the planet. Famous Daiquiri drinkers include Ernest Hemingway, who liked his doubled, and Marlene Dietrich, who drank them at the Savoy's American Bar in London.

When it comes to making a Daiquiri, hold to Charles Baker's advice in *The Gentleman's Companion*: "A too-sweet daiquiri is like a lovely lady with too much perfume." Use less sugar rather than more. Less is certainly truer to the drink's origins than the sweeter versions that eventually followed.

$1\frac{1}{2}$ oz. white rum

1 tsp. fine sugar

Juice of $1\frac{1}{2}$ small limes, strained of seeds

Place rum, sugar, and lime juice in a cocktail shaker with crushed ice and shake swiftly. Don't overmix—a good daiquiri should be ice-cold but not diluted in the least. Strain thoroughly into a cocktail glass and serve at once. Constantino Ribailagua, the legendary barman at Havana's famous La Florida bar, mixed and strained his Daiquiris so efficiently that the customer could not find a single sliver of ice in the arctic-cold drink. Other famous barmen say that the secret of a superb Daiquiri is to first dissolve the sugar in the lime juice, then add remaining ingredients, shake, and strain. If you must garnish this drink (and purists say that you should not), a twist of lime peel will do nicely.

FOR YOUR FURTHER DRINKING PLEASURE: Once the Daiquiri became popular, the Frozen Daiquiri was not far behind. To make this drink, mix and shake as above, or whir in a blender for a few seconds. Do not strain, but pour ice and all ingredients into a tall flute.

Dubonnet Cocktail

Born during Prohibition, this peerless preprandial delight was far more than a way to disguise the burn of bad gin. The flavors truly complement each other, with the herb-fortified French wine underscoring the juniper notes of the gin. Still elegant after all these years.

Where hearts are gay there's Blond Dubonnet

~Dubonnet ad, 1958

1¹/₂ oz. Dubonnet

1¹/₂ oz. gin

Twist of lemon peel

Place two or three ice cubes in a glass, add Dubonnet and gin, and mix. Strain into a chilled cocktail glass and garnish with the twist of lemon peel.

El Presidente

It was a perfect match—Americans in search of fun and rum, and Cubans with plenty of both. Old Havana must indeed have been an island paradise for those with Yankee dollars to spend, and the flavor of one famous bar, La Florida (Floridita to regulars), lives on in this recipe. While this cocktail was popular throughout Cuba, it was La Florida's famous barman, Constantino Ribailagua, who raised the drink to rare heights. His version is a bit more trouble to make than others but, we have every confidence, will be well worth your effort.

1 oz. light rum

1 oz. dry vermouth

1 tsp. grenadine

1 tsp. curaçao

Twist of orange peel

Maraschino cherry garnish

Fill a tall mixing glass with cracked ice, pour in rum and dry vermouth. Add grenadine and curaçao, stir and strain into a chilled cocktail glass. Twist orange peel over the glass so that the oil floats on the surface of the drink. Drop orange peel in, along with maraschino cherry.

French 75

Like the Tom Collins, the French 75 is another gift from the Lost Generation. Also known as a 75 Cocktail, it was named after one of the field guns used during World War I. Some historians claim that French officers quaffed it in preparation for battle, and suggest that its unavailability to enlisted men fueled dissension, and even riot, in the ranks. It was a popular offering at Harry's New York Bar in Paris for years after the war ended and, though relatively unknown today, still makes a fitting toast on Armistice Day.

1 oz. gin

Juice of 1 lemon, strained of seeds

1 tsp. powdered sugar

Champagne

We have seen two methods for making this cocktail. In the first, place gin, lemon juice, and powdered sugar in a cocktail shaker with cracked ice. Shake, strain into a chilled champagne flute, then fill with champagne. Another equally authentic method, however, is to combine the gin, lemon juice, and sugar in a mixing glass, pour into a tall glass with cracked ice, and top with champagne. For research purposes, try both.

Gibson

We take this opportunity to set the record straight: a Gibson is not a martini with an onion in it, and it was not invented in the 1940s. The original Gibson predates World War II and has nothing whatsoever to do with cocktail onions. We know this from a foray into Patrick Duffy's 1930s classic, *The Official Mixer's Manual*, which contains a recipe for the original.

At the Ashland house, where I had charge for twelve years, four barmen in spotless white, wearing carnations in their lapels, were ranged in their appointed stations behind the long, highly polished bar. When a customer approached, a little napkin of Irish linen was placed on the counter in front of him. A gleaming glass, suitable for the drink he ordered, was set before him, and the bartender then rapidly mixed his drink.

~Patrick Gavin Duffy,
THE OFFICIAL MIXER'S MANUAL, 1934

Over the years, the cocktail lost its name to the martini-like variant and had to settle for being called—when it appeared in drink books at all—a "Gibson Girl."

Another clue to the drink's age lies in its name. The leading theory is that it was first made for American artist Charles Dana Gibson at the Players Club in New York. Since Gibson died in 1944 at the age of 76, it is very likely that he drank the cocktail years before he embarked on life's greatest adventure. Drink historian Paul Harrington has gone to the admirable trouble of contacting the Players Club. While neither confirming nor denying the story of the drink's origin, the Club historian confirmed that Gibson was indeed a member from 1891 until 1903.

Here is the drink as Patrick Gavin Duffy mixed it and as Gibson himself is most likely to have drunk it. (If you're looking for the later, ginnier version, see **Gibson** as discussed under **Martini**, page 62.)

1¹/₂ oz. gin

1¹/₂ oz. dry vermouth

Maraschino cherry

Fill a mixing glass with cracked ice. Add gin and vermouth, stir, and strain into a chilled cocktail glass. Add maraschino cherry.

FOR YOUR FURTHER DRINKING PLEASURE: Numerous variations of the Gibson, made by changing the proportion and type of vermouth, range all the way down the scale to the martini-like drink that has usurped the cocktail's name. Replace the dry vermouth with sweet vermouth, add a twist of orange peel, and you have the delightfully named Gin & It, a classic before-dinner ladies' drink. Another of our favorites is the Golden Ermine, made with a generous ounce of dry vermouth and a scant half an ounce of sweet vermouth; hold the cherry.

Gimlet

We owe this drink to the lads of the British navy, who took to combining their daily rations of gin and lime juice in an effort to stave off boredom and scurvy at the same time. The drink, which seems to have gotten its name from the corkscrew-like device used to tap kegs of lime juice, was initially ignored in the Colonies. However, it became a staple throughout the farthest reaches of the British empire. Writing in the 1930s, Charles Baker laments the Gimlet's "unheralded" status in the U.S., noting that "throughout the whole swing of the Far East, starting with Bombay—down the Malabar Coast to Colombo; to Penang, Singapore, Hong Kong and Shanghai, the Gimlet is just as well known as our Martini here." The Far East Gimlet, as drunk by Baker and others, was diluted with water and served in a large champagne saucer.

A real Gimlet is
half gin and half Rose's
lime juice, and nothing else.
It beats martinis hollow.

~Raymond Chandler,
THE LONG GOODBYE, 1953

Other American recipes, stemming from the 1920s and '30s, call for club soda instead of water.

Despite Baker's valiant attempts to popularize the Gimlet, the cocktail didn't really catch on in the States until Raymond Chandler's fictional detective, Philip Marlowe, imbued it with a certain *noir chic.* Now stripped of water and soda, the cocktail had a macho flair just right for those bent on sex and self-destruction. It's been a hit ever since.

Gimlet

1¹/₂ oz. gin
¹/₂ oz. Rose's lime juice
Lime-wedge garnish

While most prefer this cocktail on the rocks, a few prefer it straight up. If mixing the former, add gin and Rose's lime to an old-fashioned glass filled with ice. Stir and serve with lime wedge in the drink, not perched on the rim of the glass. For those who prefer their Gimlets without ice, stir gin and Rose's lime together in a mixing glass filled with ice, strain into a cocktail glass, and add garnish.

One final note: our recipe calls for a 3:1 ration of gin to Rose's, but this is only a suggestion. We have seen recipes calling for everything from 1:1 to 4:1 ratios, suggesting that the Gimlet's gin-to-Rose's issue is at least as tempestuous as the Martini's never-to-be-settled gin-to-vermouth controversy. We recommend that you undertake your own rigorous testing to determine your preferred balance.

Highball

The true highball, as created by New York bartender Patrick Gavin Duffy in the 1890s, consisted of just two ingredients: one spirit and one mixer. This relatively potent combination earned the drink its name—in railroad signal talk, a raised ball on a pole was a sign for the engineer to speed up. And as any drinker of highballs will tell you, there is a definite element of speed at work in this drink. Duffy's preferred mixer was club soda, but over the years, water, ginger ale, and flavored sodas also came into use. In the 1930s, it became fashionable to add a dash of a third ingredient, such as bitters or grenadine. However, we decry this flourish. The splendid thing about a highball is its elegant simplicity. Learn to quaff a highball and you'll be at ease anywhere.

1$\frac{1}{2}$ oz. liquor

Mixer

Place several ice cubes in a highball glass and add liquor, then mixer. Although highballs are served with a stirrer, overmixing is a faux pas. A highball should not present a single, monotonal flavor but varying shades of taste as one drinks. Note that a gin and tonic shouldn't be stirred at all, leaving the gin to hover beneath an arctic canopy of ice and tonic.

Seven Classic Highballs

GIN AND GINGER The drier the ginger ale in this drink, the better. Garnish with a twist of lemon peel.

GIN AND TONIC Before adding ingredients, rub a wedge of lime around the rim of the glass. Add gin, lime wedge, and tonic; serve. While the original drink was, like the DAIQUIRI (see page 36), medicinal, it proved so popular that the Vodka and Tonic and the Rum and Tonic soon followed. NOTE: This is one highball that shouldn't be stirred.

HORSE'S NECK The original version of this highball, circa 1910, called for bourbon and ginger ale. Later guides often feature a choice of spirits,

including blended whiskey and brandy. No matter what spirit you use, the WOW of this drink comes from the continuous, spiral-cut peel of an entire lemon streaming from the rim of the glass to the very bottom.

IRISH COOLER (Also known as an Irish Buck.) To Irish whiskey, add club soda and a spiral-cut lemon peel à la Horse's Neck, above.

RUM AND COKE Still one of the world's most popular drinks. Please use authentic Coca-Cola and nothing but. After all these years, it's still the real thing. Garnish with lime.

SCOTCH AND SODA The *sine qua non* of highballs, which shouldn't be spoiled with a garnish.

7 & 7 A classic composed of Seagram's 7-Crown Whiskey and 7-Up.

Gimme a whiskey, ginger ale on the side . . . and don't be stingy, baby!

~Greta Garbo in

ANNA CHRISTIE, 1930

48

HOP TO IT...

Enjoy that Bright Morning Taste Today!

You'll take to the Bright Morning Taste of Schenley Reserve with your first cool sip of a Schenley-and-Soda. Every drop is at the *peak* of *pre-war quality*. Ask for it today.

They also serve who BUY and HOLD War Bonds

SCHENLEY
Reserve

PRE-WAR QUALITY

Long Island Iced Tea

We have no doubt that many a Long Island lady sipped this sassy cooler between rounds of golf and sets of tennis and during afternoons of bridge. Nothing strong for me, please, I'll just have a little more of that lovely iced tea.

2 tsp. Cointreau

2 tsp. gin

2 tsp. vodka

2 tsp. white rum

2 tsp. tequila

Juice of 1 lime, strained of seeds

Cola

Lime-wheel garnish

Place several ice cubes in a highball glass. Add Cointreau, gin, vodka, rum, tequila, and lime juice. Stir gently, fill to the brim with chilled cola, and garnish with a lime wheel.

Mai Tai

Tahitian it may be in name and spirit, but the first Mai Tai was made by Victor (Trader Vic) Bergeron in Emeryville, California, around 1944. According to fairly well documented accounts, Vic was manning the bar at his restaurant, Hinky Dink's, when two Tahitian friends asked him to whip up something unusual. Bergeron did so, and, after tasting the unique concoction, his friends raised their glasses in tribute and enthusiastically called out "Mai tai! Roa ae!"—loosely translated as "the best damn thing we've ever drunk!"

Bergeron's original drink is indeed a master composition of sweet and sharp flavors. Unfortunately, the complex recipe was soon corrupted by lazy or hurried bartenders who turned this wonderful cocktail into a kind of sweet spiked punch. While it takes some doing to gather the ingredients for an authentic Mai Tai, we can't think of a more noble endeavor—or one with lovelier results.

HE: I envy people who drink. At least they know what to blame everything on.
SHE: If it's so simple, why don't you drink?

~Oscar Levant and Joan Crawford in
HUMORESQUE, 1946

Mai Tai

1 oz. light rum

1 oz. dark rum

$^1/_2$ oz. curaçao

$1^1/_2$ tsp. rock-candy syrup or simple syrup

$1^1/_2$ tsp. orgeat (almond) syrup

Lime peel

Mint sprig

Place rums, curaçao, and syrups in a cocktail shaker with cracked ice. Shake, strain into a chilled old-fashioned glass, and garnish with lime and mint. Serve with a straw and a stirrer.

Manhattan

As glam as the island that shares the name, this thoroughly American drink is one of the few classics made with whiskey rather than clear spirits. By all accounts, this cocktail was invented at New York's Manhattan Club in the last years of the nineteenth century. There, however, agreement ends and two stories vie for our attention. One history traces the drink's origin to 1874, when Jennie Jerome Churchill threw a party at the club to celebrate Samuel Tilden's successful run for governor. A second story, popularized in John Mariani's *The Dictionary of American Food and Drink*, suggests that the drink was first made at the Club some years later for a Supreme Court justice named Truax. There are problems with both stories. Although Tilden was indeed elected in 1874, it's unlikely that Jennie was doing much entertaining—on November 30, she was at home in Blenheim Castle, England, giving birth to the future Sir Winston. The second story is also difficult to authenticate. There has never been a U.S. Supreme Court justice named Truax. Although there is a New York Supreme Court, it is presided over by judges, not justices, and we have been unable to verify Truax's presence there. Clearly, we must revive ourselves with several more of these delicious cocktails before we are ready to set forth, once more, on the difficult and arduous research trail.

Classic Manhattan

1$\frac{1}{2}$ oz. rye

$\frac{3}{4}$ oz. sweet vermouth

2 dashes Angostura bitters

Maraschino cherry

Place cracked ice in a cocktail shaker and add rye (or bourbon or blended whiskey), vermouth, and bitters. Shake, strain into a chilled cocktail glass, and add cherry. To make a Dry Manhattan, use dry vermouth instead of sweet, and garnish with a twist of lemon peel and an olive instead of a cherry. For a Perfect Manhattan, use $\frac{3}{8}$ oz. (2$\frac{1}{4}$ tsp.) each of sweet and dry vermouth.

FOR YOUR FURTHER DRINKING PLEASURE: There are endless drinks based on the appealing combination of whiskey and vermouth, including the Hot Deck Cocktail, a Classic Manhattan made with Jamaican ginger instead of bitters (hold the cherry), and the Brooklyn Cocktail, a Dry Manhattan with one dash each of maraschino and Amer Picon (a variety of French bitters) taking the place of Angostura bitters. To make a New 1920 Cocktail, use 1$\frac{1}{2}$ oz. rye, increase the amount of sweet and dry vermouth to $\frac{3}{4}$ oz. each, add a dash of orange bitters, and serve with a twist of lemon peel.

Margarita

Few remember Marjorie King, siren of the silent screen, but her allergy lives on. As a guest at Danny Herrera's splendid Rancha La Gloria in Tijuana in the 1930s, Marjorie confessed that she was allergic to virtually every type of liquor except tequila. Her host responded by creating a cocktail to meet the challenge and giving it the Spanish version of his guest's name.

The raging debate in contemporary Margaritaland is whether to make the cocktail with lime juice only, or a combination of lime and lemon. We'd like to say that the lime-only version is the original, since it's the version we prefer, but we can't make this declaration. Lemon is at least as traditional as lime, and shots of tequila were originally drunk with a preceding bite into a lemon wedge rather than a wedge of lime. So we leave it to you to suit yourself on this score. Whatever you decide to do, though, please don't omit the Cointreau (or triple sec)—the compatibility of tequila and orange has been vastly underappreciated.

HE: What is a cocktail dress? SHE: Something to spill cocktails on.

~William Powell and Jean Arthur in THE EX-MRS. BRADFORD, 1936

55

Margarita

Lime wedge

Salt

1$\frac{1}{2}$ oz. tequila

Juice of one large lime, strained of seeds

$\frac{1}{2}$ oz. Cointreau (triple sec is an acceptable substitute)

Rub the rim of a chilled cocktail glass with a wedge of lime and dip rim in a saucer of salt to make salt adhere. Place tequila, lime juice, and Cointreau (or triple sec) in a cocktail shaker with cracked ice. Shake swiftly and strain into the prepared glass.

FOR YOUR FURTHER DRINKING PLEASURE: To make a Frozen Margarita, use very finely cracked or crushed ice. Mix and shake as above, or whir in a blender for a few seconds. Do not strain, but pour ice and all into a goblet.

Martini

Success may have many fathers, but not nearly as many as the goddess of all cocktails, the incomparable martini. We hear that it was invented by "Professor" Jerry Thomas of San Francisco's Occidental Hotel, who mixed it for a gold miner who was on his way to the nearby town of Martinez. We hear that it originated in the town of Martinez and was first mixed by a bartender named Richelieu. We hear that it was invented by Martini di Arma di Traggi, bartender at New York's Knickerbocker Hotel. We hear that the Brits invented it and named it after the Martini & Henry rifle, used by the British army from 1871 to 1891. Not only have we found it impossible to untangle and examine the veracity of these tales, but we've discovered that doing so cuts into valuable drinking time.

The first Martini, or Martinez, as it was often called, was a far cry from the desert-dry drink we know today. Early recipes invariably used Old Tom gin, a sweet version of the spirit, and sweet rather

NORA: Now, how many drinks have you had?
NICK: This will make six martinis.
NORA (to waiter): All right. Will you bring me five more martinis? Line them right up here.

~Myrna Loy and William Powell
in THE THIN MAN, 1934

than dry vermouth. Early recipes also had nearly equal amounts of gin to vermouth, and sweetened the drink further with syrup, maraschino or orange liqueur, and a squeeze of lemon. By 1900, the drink, now universally known as a Martini, had become less sweet. Syrup and liqueurs were omitted from the recipe, and dry gin and vermouth were used in place of sweet. An effort was made to distinguish between the earlier sweet cocktail and the drier version by giving the new drink a different name—both "Marguerite" and "Puritan" were tried, but neither caught on, and people simply asked for a Dry Martini instead.

Throughout the first half of the century, the Martini continued its rise to the top. Every event that should have diminished the drink's popularity—

SALES MANAGER

Intangible experience, must be able to move effectively at top management level and understand "Big Business" problems. Should be able to handle twelve martinis.

Drink Up

~want ad, NEW YORK TIMES, 1956

58

Prohibition, the Depression, two world wars—only increased its status. It was the drink that allowed Hemingway's hero to momentarily forget the carnage of World War I in *A Farewell To Arms*, and the first post-Prohibition drink served by FDR in the White House. As the Depression eased, it became a glamorous promise of good times to come. Even a lady could knock back a slew of them without losing a shred of elegance, as Myrna Loy proved in 1934's *The Thin Man*. From the ashes of World War II, the Martini emerged as sleek and fresh as Dior's New Look, and seemed poised to continue its reign. But while the drink had thrived through cycles of adversity, peace and prosperity took a heavy toll on its popularity. In the 1950s, belting back the potent cocktail, now drier and ginnier than ever, became a prerequisite job skill for the corporate climb. The Martini's libertine sparkle dissolved in a cloud of gray flannel and its icily sublime taste became an endangered species, a turn of events that must have had even Asta spinning in his grave.

Sweet Martini

1 oz. sweet gin
1 oz. sweet vermouth
1 dash orange bitters
1 dash curaçao
Twist of lemon peel

The affliction that is cutting down the productive time in the office and destroying the benign temper of most of the bartenders is the thing called the very dry martini. It is a mass madness, a cult, a frenzy, a body of folklore, a mystique, an expertise of a sort that may well earn for this decade the name of the Numb (or Glazed) Fifties. . . . Along every stretch of polished mahogany in public places and in countless living rooms, there is no talk of the world crisis. . . only of how to get a martini really dry.

~C. B. Palmer in the NEW YORK TIMES, 1952

59

Martini Timeline

1860S The first forerunners of the Martini are mixed.

1884 THE MODERN BARTENDER'S GUIDE by O. H. Byron features a recipe for a drink called a "martinez," describing it as a Manhattan made with gin instead of whiskey.

1888 The name "Martini" appears in print for the first time in the NEW AND IMPROVED ILLUSTRATED BARTENDER'S MANUAL by Harry Johnson. Gin to vermouth ratio: 1:1.

1891 COCKTAIL BOOTHBY'S AMERICAN BARTENDER endorses a drier Martini by omitting the syrup.

1894 Heublein Company offers a Martini that is premixed.

1896 IN FANCY DRINKS AND HOW TO MIX THEM, Thomas Stuart provides the first recipe for a dry Martini. Calling the new drink a "Marguerite," Stuart introduces dry gin and vermouth.

C. 1898 A drink called the "Puritan" is introduced. Like the Marguerite, it is essentially a dried-out Martini.

1900-10 The dry Martini replaces the original as the standard version of the drink. Sales of Noilly Prat, a popular brand of dry vermouth, jump from 25,000 cases a year to three times that number.

1904 Martinis are well known enough for O. Henry to mention them, without explanation, in his story "THE GENTLE GRAFTER."

1914 As World War I rages, the Martini is America's number-one cocktail, known throughout the world as the symbol of all things civilized.

1917 The NEW YORK SUN playfully unearths the ancient Egyptian god of thirst, Dri Mart Ini.

1920S Prohibition adds to the Martini's popularity as easy-to-make bathtub gin sloshes all across the nation.

1933 With the end of Prohibition, President Roosevelt serves legal Martinis in the White House.

1940s Gin to vermouth ratio: 2:1.

1941 Writer Sherwood Anderson dies after accidentally swallowing the toothpick in the olive. The popularity of toothpicks abruptly declines.

1943 As the Allies meet to discuss the defeat of the Axis, Roosevelt offers Stalin a celebratory Martini. Stalin assents but complains that he finds the drink "cold on the stomach."

Why don't you get out of that wet coat and into a dry martini?

~Robert Benchley as Major Osborne in THE MAJOR AND THE MINOR, 1942

1944 With the Liberation of Paris, Ernest Hemingway and several soldiers place an order for 73 Martinis at the bar of the swank Hotel Ritz.

1950s The three-martini lunch becomes *de rigueur* for organization men everywhere. Gin to vermouth ratio: 3:1.

1951 A recipe for the vodkatini appears in Ted Saucier's BOTTOMS UP.

Medium Martini

2 oz. gin

$\frac{1}{2}$–1 oz. dry vermouth

Olive garnish

Dry Martini

$2\frac{1}{2}$ oz. gin

1 tbsp. dry vermouth

Olive garnish

Ultradry Martini

$2\frac{1}{2}$ oz. gin

1 tsp. dry vermouth

Olive garnish

As these recipes suggest, the dryness of a Martini (gin to vermouth ratio) is very much a matter of individual taste, and Martinis have become ever drier over the decades. A dry Martini of the 1930s would be considered awash in vermouth by today's standards. However, even in the golden age, a few enthusiasts liked theirs extra-dry, including Churchill, who made his by pouring out the gin and "glancing briefly at a bottle of vermouth." FDR, who liked his with somewhat more vermouth, preferred a Dirty Martini, made by adding a few drops of olive juice.

61

Dryness and individual preference aside, the key ingredient in a superlative Martini is neither gin nor vermouth, but temperature. Icy coldness is a must, and we recommend storing both gin and glasses in the freezer. To mix a Martini, place ingredients in a metal shaker along with cracked ice. Stir gently and strain into a chilled cocktail glass. Though the olive has become the ubiquitous garnish of choice, a small spiral of lemon peel is an acceptable and refreshing alternative.

FOR YOUR FURTHER DRINKING PLEASURE: One cannot discuss the Martini without mentioning two related cocktails. To make a Vodkatini, follow the proportions for a dry or ultradry Martini as taste dictates, replacing the gin with vodka and garnishing with either an olive or a twist of lemon peel. In discussing the Martini, one must also mention the Gibson. Strictly speaking, a Gibson is not a Martini but a drink in its own right (see page 42). However, modernists have thrown the Gibson's individuality to the winds, and the contemporary Gibson is a dry (or ultradry) Martini garnished with a pearl cocktail onion rather than an olive. To add to the confusion, some add both olive and onion.

Mint Julep

Like the United States, the julep is a melting pot. Its name comes from the Arab *julab* (sweet rose water), while its approach resembles that of a South American **Crusta** (see page 26), and, while there's no consensus on an "original" recipe, the results are always uniquely and indisputably North American.

The earliest recorded mention of this southern refresher dates back to 1803, when a British tutor working in the South described it as a drink "taken by Virginians of a morning." Another Brit, Captain Frederick Maryatt, took the recipe back to England with him, noting that the drink was irresistible when the temperature was 100 but could "be drunk with equal satisfaction when the thermometer is as low as 70 degrees." Maryatt's recipe, like many early versions, relied on cognac and brandy. As the South refined production of its own distinctive liquor, bourbon replaced imported spirits in the drink. Despite vigorous debates over the drink's proper constituents, it was the bourbon version that was served at the Kentucky Derby around 1875, and the bourbon version that became the Derby's official drink in the late 1930s.

Bourbon Mint Julep

2 tsp. sugar

2 tbsp. water

6–8 sprigs of fresh mint

4 oz. bourbon

Place sugar and water in a mixing glass and muddle until sugar is completely dissolved. Add all but one sprig of mint, and crush slightly to release the fragrance. Let stand a few minutes, then transfer to a frosted collins glass or silver cup (the traditional vessel for juleps). Fill the glass partially with crushed ice. Add bourbon, stir once, then add enough additional ice to fill the glass. Garnish with the reserved mint.

Georgia Mint Julep

1 tsp. powdered sugar

1 tbsp. water

10–12 sprigs of fresh mint

2 oz. cognac

2 oz. peach brandy

Peach slice for garnish

Follow the mixing method for the Bourbon Mint Julep, above. Garnish with a slice of fresh peach.

FOR YOUR FURTHER DRINKING PLEASURE: One of our favorite versions of the julep is the Manila Hotel Mint Julep, as served in Luzon, Philippines, in 1926. To make it, follow the directions for a Bourbon Mint Julep but finish by floating 2 teaspoons of rum on top and garnishing with two sticks of fresh pineapple.

First among fine whiskies

THREE FEATHERS

Reserve

RESERVE

Old Fashioned

You have to be pretty swell for Cole Porter to have written a song about you, and "Make It Another Old-Fashioned, Please," from 1940's *Panama Hattie*, is only one reason to celebrate this drink. Invented by whiskey distiller Colonel James Pepper and the bartender of the Pendennis Club in Louisville around 1900, the Old-Fashioned soon became a fixture from New York to Waikiki. Lest you think the fruit is a recent addition, let us assure you that it is found in the earliest recipes. Only the cherry was added later, when technology made possible the mass production of maraschino cherries in the 1920s.

1 sugar cube
2 dashes Angostura bitters
Club soda

$1^1/_2$ oz. bourbon (rye or blended whiskey may be used instead)
1 slice orange peel

1 slice lemon peel
1 slice pineapple
Maraschino cherry

Place sugar cube in an old-fashioned glass and soak it with bitters. Add just enough club soda to cover the sugar, then muddle until the cube is completely dissolved. Add cracked ice, bourbon, orange and lemon peels, pineapple, and cherry. Finish with a splash of club soda and serve with a swizzle stick.

VARIATION: We have also seen early recipes that include a dash or 2 of curaçao.

Pegu Club Cocktail

One of the chief, if unsung, achievements of the British colonial era was putting good gin into the hands of people who knew how to use it. And one of the results was this delightful cocktail, born in the 1930s at the Pegu Club, outside Rangoon. Within a decade, it became one of the most popular drinks anywhere in the world. We urge a rediscovery of this forgotten beauty, and are prepared to drink a hundred of them on the Capitol steps, if need be, to draw attention to our cause. We'll have legions of followers in no time.

> We shall drink to our partnership. Do you like gin? It is my only weakness.
>
> ~Ernest Thesiger as Dr. Pretorius in THE BRIDE OF FRANKENSTEIN, 1935

$1\frac{1}{2}$ oz. gin

$3/_4$ oz. curaçao

1 dash Angostura bitters

1 dash orange bitters

Juice of $1/_2$ lime, strained of seeds

Place all ingredients in a mixing glass with cracked ice. Stir well and strain into a chilled cocktail glass.

Pink Gin

A blend of soul-soothing gin and stomach-soothing bitters, this drink became a favorite in India among British officers whose systems found the food, water, and climate there more than a little unsettling. While most recipes simply ask you to combine the ingredients, we much prefer the elegant method described below. Drink it, and think of the Raj.

4–5 dashes Angostura bitters

2 oz. gin

Twist of lemon peel

Shake 4 or 5 dashes of bitters into a chilled cocktail glass. Tip the glass, rolling from side to side, until the bitters coat the inside of the glass. Pour off excess. Gently pour gin into the glass, add a piece of cracked ice if desired, and garnish with a slim twist of lemon peel.

FOR YOUR FURTHER DRINKING PLEASURE: Pink Gin is the simplest and most famous of several drinks based on the winning combination of gin and bitters. Here are six others well worth the effort.

ALASKA   Place 2 oz. gin, $^1/_2$ oz. yellow chartreuse, and 2 dashes orange bitters in a mixing glass. Add cracked ice, stir, and strain into a chilled cocktail glass. Garnish with a twist of lemon.

ANGLER   Place 2 oz. gin, 2 dashes grenadine, 3 dashes Angostura bitters, and 3 dashes orange bitters in a mixing glass with 2 ice cubes. Stir and strain into a chilled cocktail glass.

ASTORIA   Place $1^1/_2$ oz. gin, $^3/_4$ oz. dry vermouth, and a dash of orange bitters in a mixing glass. Add cracked ice, stir, and strain into a chilled cocktail glass. Garnish with a stuffed olive.

BENNETT   Place $1^1/_2$ oz. gin, strained juice of $^1/_2$ lime, 1 tsp. powdered sugar, and 2 dashes Angostura bitters in a cocktail shaker with cracked ice. Shake and strain into a chilled cocktail glass.

BLENTON   Place $1^1/_2$ oz. gin, $^3/_4$ oz. sweet vermouth, and a dash of Angostura bitters in a mixing glass. Add cracked ice, stir, and strain into a chilled cocktail glass. Garnish with a cherry and a twist of lemon peel.

BLUE BIRD   Place $1^1/_2$ oz. gin, 5 dashes curaçao, and 4 dashes Angostura bitters in a mixing glass. Add cracked ice, stir, and strain into a chilled cock-tail glass. Garnish with a cherry and a twist of lemon peel.

Pousse-Café

In *The Gentleman's Companion*, Charles Baker describes a night in Calcutta in 1926 when he and his host decided to "get every cordial and liqueur in the place, and brew bigger and better pousse-cafés—and each time one went bad, the culprit responsible had to toss it off, bottoms up. When a successful one was brewed with five layers or more, the result was shared….[T]his sort of thing only goes to show what grown men will do to keep from devoting their time to something constructive in life." Well, yes—but we can't think of a lovelier waste of time than the Pousse-café.

The Pousse-café (literally, "coffee pusher") is the most spectacular of after-dinner drinks. Like the Jazz Age itself, this drink is a vibrant, even gaudy, array of flavors and colors. Various ingredients, both alcoholic and non, can go into the drink. The idea is to float multiple layers atop one another so artfully that each stratum remains sharply separate from its neighbors. When properly done, the result is a rainbow in a glass, containing as few as two bands or as many as seven.

Those who wish to become masters of the Pousse-café need two things: the ability to float one ingredient atop another (see page 9) and a knowledge of the relative weight of each ingredient. The heaviest liquid must always go into the glass first, working up to the lightest. If you are a beginner, refine your technique by floating heavy cream atop Kahlúa, then move on to these delightful and colorful combinations.

Fourth of July

Grenadine

Cointreau

Blue curaçao

French Tricolor

Grenadine

Maraschino

Crème Yvette

Jersey Lily

Green Chartreuse

Cognac

Angostura bitters:
10 drops

Angel's Blush

Maraschino

Crème Yvette

Benedictine

Heavy cream

Liquid Symphony

Crème de rose

Yellow Chartreuse

Green crème de menthe

Brandy

Paris Rainbow

Crème de violette

Crème de cassis

Maraschino

Green crème de menthe

Yellow Chartreuse

Curaçao

Cherry brandy

Havana Rainbow

Grenadine

Anisette

Parfait amour

Green crème de menthe

Yellow curaçao

Yellow Chartreuse

Rum

Float ingredients in a stemmed glass in the order given, using equal amounts of each liqueur to fill the glass. It's highly desirable to consider the capacity of the glass you are using, so that you can determine how much of each ingredient will be needed and measure appropriately. Keep in mind that no layer should be too deep—you should be able to drink through each layer to taste the one below. Pousse-cafés may be made ahead of time and refrigerated.

If a layer isn't as crisp as it should be when you first pour it, wait a moment and gravity will separate the heavier liquid from the lighter. After the layer has settled, proceed with the next.

Ramos Fizz

Every cloud has its silver lining, and Prohibition's gift to the world is the recipe for this froth of ginny delight. Invented by Enrico Ramos, owner of the Imperial Cabinet Saloon in New Orleans, the formula was a very well-guarded secret until 1920. When the feds shut down the place and padlocked the doors, Enrico's brother Charles became so outraged that he began freely dispensing the recipe he had hitherto kept so jealously. *Laissez les bons temps rouler!*

1^1/$_2$ oz. gin

Juice of ^{1}/$_2$ lemon, strained of seeds

Juice of ^{1}/$_2$ lime, strained of seeds

3 dashes orange-flower water

1 egg white*

1^1/$_2$ oz. cream

1 tsp. sugar

Splash of club soda (optional)

Mint-sprig or lime-wedge garnish

Place all ingredients except club soda in a shaker with cracked ice. Shake for 5–12 minutes. This is the secret of a truly exceptional Ramos Fizz, and those

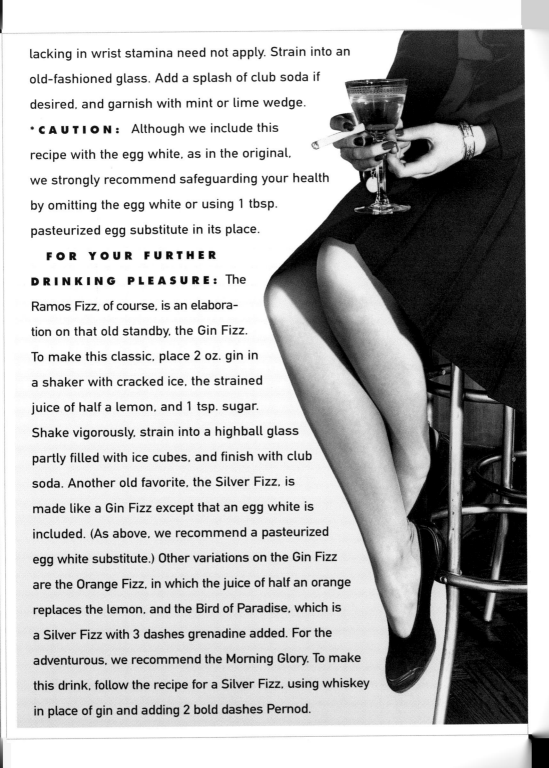

lacking in wrist stamina need not apply. Strain into an old-fashioned glass. Add a splash of club soda if desired, and garnish with mint or lime wedge.

*CAUTION: Although we include this recipe with the egg white, as in the original, we strongly recommend safeguarding your health by omitting the egg white or using 1 tbsp. pasteurized egg substitute in its place.

FOR YOUR FURTHER DRINKING PLEASURE: The Ramos Fizz, of course, is an elaboration on that old standby, the Gin Fizz. To make this classic, place 2 oz. gin in a shaker with cracked ice, the strained juice of half a lemon, and 1 tsp. sugar. Shake vigorously, strain into a highball glass partly filled with ice cubes, and finish with club soda. Another old favorite, the Silver Fizz, is made like a Gin Fizz except that an egg white is included. (As above, we recommend a pasteurized egg white substitute.) Other variations on the Gin Fizz are the Orange Fizz, in which the juice of half an orange replaces the lemon, and the Bird of Paradise, which is a Silver Fizz with 3 dashes grenadine added. For the adventurous, we recommend the Morning Glory. To make this drink, follow the recipe for a Silver Fizz, using whiskey in place of gin and adding 2 bold dashes Pernod.

Rickeys

Similar to the Collins and the Fizz, the Rickey is a brisk, tart refresher, but one that omits the sugar. A product of the 1890s, this cocktail was born at Shoemaker's Restaurant in Washington, D.C., and gets its name from lobbyist Joe Rickey, for whom the bartender first made it. Had there been personal income tax at the time, Joe and the bartender might have written the gin and soda off as a business expense. As it is, we'll drink to their honor.

1½ oz. gin

Juice of 1 lime, strained of seeds

Club soda

Lime-wedge garnish

Place ice cubes in a highball glass, then add gin and lime juice. Top with club soda, stir gently, and garnish with lime wedge.

VARIATIONS: Sadly, the Gin Rickey has become the only well-known form of this wonderfully simple drink. It was not always so. In his 1934 drink guide, THE OFFICIAL MIXER'S MANUAL, Patrick Duffy lists a baker's dozen types, of which the Gin Rickey is only one. The other twelve are:

AMER PICON RICKEY

APPLEJACK RICKEY

APRICOT RICKEY (APRICOT LIQUEUR)

BOURBON RICKEY

CORDIAL (ANY TYPE) RICKEY

GRENADINE RICKEY

IRISH RICKEY (IRISH WHISKEY)

RASPBERRY RICKEY (RASPBERRY LIQUEUR)

RUM RICKEY

RYE RICKEY

SCOTCH RICKEY

SLOE GIN RICKEY

FOR YOUR FURTHER DRINKING PLEASURE: The above drinks are made exactly like the given recipe except for the main ingredient. A slightly more elaborate drink is the Savoy Hotel Rickey, which is a Gin Rickey with 4 dashes of grenadine added. Reduce the grenadine to 2 dashes, add a slice of pineapple, and you have a Hugo Rickey. Return to the original Gin Rickey recipe, add 2 dashes raspberry syrup, and you have a Porto Rico Rickey. All three of these are worth a few extra twists of the wrist, and we recommend them for your more playful moods.

Rob Roy

We aren't quite sure when this drink dates from—certainly not from eighteenth-century Scotland, as rebel leader Rob Roy himself did. None of our pre–World War II drink guides includes this cocktail, but it does appear in the *Esquire Drink Book* of 1956. Other than the link of scotch to Scot, color may have had much to do with the naming of this drink. It's smoky auburn hue reminds us that Rob Roy's real surname was Macgregor, with the nickname "Roy" given to denote his wild red hair.

I should have never switched from scotch to martinis.

~Humphrey Bogart's last words

1¹/₂ oz. scotch

³/₄ oz. sweet vermouth

2 dashes Angostura bitters

Maraschino cherry garnish (optional)

Pour scotch and sweet vermouth into a mixing glass with cracked ice. Add bitters, stir, and strain into a chilled cocktail glass into which the cherry has

already been placed. As with other drinks that combine spirits with vermouth, the ratio in the Rob Roy is subject to variation. We recommend the version mixed at the Waldorf-Astoria Hotel in the mid-1950s, with 3 parts scotch to 1 part vermouth, and a twist of lemon peel rather than a Maraschino cherry garnish.

FOR YOUR FURTHER DRINKING PLEASURE: While the Rob Roy seems to be no older than the cold war, we found several forerunners that have much in common with it. A stylish drink from the 1920s, the Affinity, combines sweet and dry vermouth with scotch. To make it, combine 1 oz. sweet vermouth, 1 oz. dry vermouth, and 1 oz. scotch in a cocktail shaker with ice; add a dash of Angostura bitters, then shake and strain into a cocktail glass. Twist a bit of lemon peel over the glass, but do not add it to the drink.

The Russians: Black and White

Isn't it strange that one of the most popular after-dinner drinks of the Cold War era was the Black Russian? Perhaps not. We can't think of a better way to soothe atomic jitters than with these smoothly syrupy kickers.

Black Russian

$1^1/_2$ oz. vodka

$^3/_4$ oz. Kahlúa

Place ice cubes in an old-fashioned glass. Pour in vodka first, then Kahlúa. Stir gently and serve with a swizzle stick.

White Russian

$1^1/_2$ oz. vodka

$^3/_4$ oz. Kahlúa

$^3/_4$ oz. heavy cream

Place ice cubes in an old-fashioned glass. Pour in vodka first, then Kahlúa, and stir gently. Float cream on top and serve with a swizzle stick.

FOR YOUR FURTHER DRINKING PLEASURE: The White Russian, born in the 1950s, actually has an ancestor that dates back to the 1920s—the Barbara. To make this cocktail, follow the directions for a White Russian but replace the Kahlúa with crème de cacao.

Sazerac

As full of dusky legend as the New Orleans streets where it was born, the original Sazerac called for cognac and absinthe. In all probability, it was first brewed in the 1830s by Antoine A. Peychaud, best known to tipplers for inventing Peychaud's bitters. In the 1850s, a local coffeehouse made its own version of the drink, naming it Sazerac, after the brand

I lived near the main street of the quarter which is named Royal. Down this street, running on the same tracks, are two streetcars, one named Desire and the other named Cemetery. The indiscourage-able [sic] progress up and down Royal struck me as having some symbolic bearing of a broad nature on life in the Vieux Carré—and everywhere else, for that matter.

~Tennessee Williams, 1940

of imported French brandy from which it was made. Eventually, the coffeehouse re-named itself after the drink as well. Rye whiskey replaced im-ported Sazerac brandy as an ingredient shortly after the Civil War, and Pernod came in as a replacement for absinthe, which was banned in 1912. Despite these changes, the Sazerac has endured, though not always in uncor-rupted form. Many drink manuals call for a sugar cube and water, while modern manuals that we checked advised the addition of club soda. Heavens! In the interest of historical preservation, we offer here the recipe and method as mixed and drunk at the Sazerac in the early 1930s.

3 or 4 dashes Pernod
(120 proof
preferable)
2 oz. rye (or bourbon or
blended whiskey)
3 or 4 hearty
dashes Peychaud bitters
Long, thin twist of
lemon peel

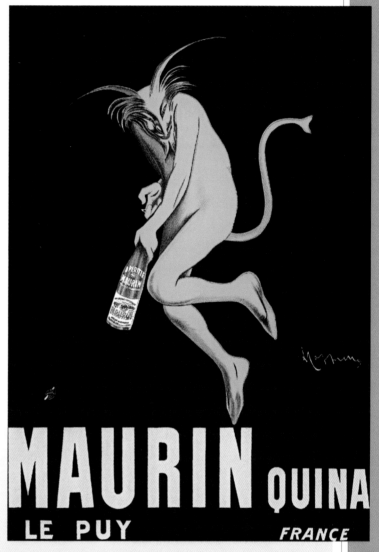

Place Pernod in a well-chilled old-fashioned glass. Tilt the glass to coat sides completely. Pour off any excess Pernod. Place rye and Peychaud bitters into a cocktail shaker with several ice cubes. Shake for a good 30 seconds and strain into prepared glass. Twist the peel over the drink, then drop it in gently.

Screwdriver

Technically, the Screwdriver is a highball—but such an influential one that it transcends the category. Like many vodka drinks, it is relatively recent, dating back to just the 1950s. According to popular lore, this drink owes its name to an American oilman in Iran. When he found himself without a swizzle stick for his vodka and orange juice, he did the job with a screwdriver. The catchy name catapulted the drink to mass popularity, making it a brunchtime and lunchtime favorite with all those who prefer a little nourishment with their o.j.

2 oz. vodka

Freshly squeezed orange juice

Slice of orange

Place 2 or 3 ice cubes in a highball glass, add vodka, then fill with orange juice. Stir. Garnish with orange slice and serve with swizzle stick.

FOR YOUR FURTHER DRINKING PLEASURE: Two other vodka-and-juice classics deserve mention: the Cape Codder, a Screwdriver in which cranberry juice is used in place of orange juice and takes a lime slice for garnish; and the Sea Breeze, a refreshing cocktail, that uses 2 oz. vodka, equal parts cranberry and grapefruit juices, and a lime-slice garnish.

Sidecar

It can get chilly riding in the sidecar of a chauffeur-driven motorcycle. Which is why one World War I officer, on being dropped off at his favorite Parisian boîte, requested a warming drink from the bartender. Whether the boîte in question was Harry's or the Ritz remains in lively dispute, and we can't say we blame any establishment for claiming authorship of this lovely cocktail. The only thing that arouses our anger is the tendency of various bartenders over the years to sully the original pristine proportions of this drink with corrupting "innovations," such as substituting triple sec for Cointreau, using lime juice or—even worse—sour mix instead of lemon, and fiddling with the proportions so recklessly that the drink is no longer recognizable. We deplore these enhancements, and return to the authentic recipe and proportions.

$1^1/_2$ oz. brandy

$^3/_4$ oz. Cointreau

$^3/_4$ oz. lemon juice, strained of seeds

Combine ingredients in a shaker with cracked ice. Shake vigorously and strain into a chilled cocktail glass.

Silver Bullet

Once upon a time, before vodka's unfriendly takeover of so many classic clear recipes, the Silver Bullet was a gin drink. It should be so again—it's a lovely reason to keep another vintage classic, kümmel, on hand.

1 1/2 oz. gin

3/4 oz. kümmel

3/4 oz. lemon juice, strained of seeds

Place ingredients in mixing glass with cracked ice. Stir, then strain into a chilled cocktail glass. Please note that the Silver Bullet, even in today's gone-Hollywood era, is served without garnish.

VARIATION: To make a contemporary Silver Bullet, simply replace the gin with a like amount of vodka.

FOR YOUR FURTHER DRINKING PLEASURE: A close cousin to the classic Silver Bullet is the Silver Streak. To make it, combine 1 1/2 oz. each of gin and kümmel in a mixing glass with cracked ice, stir, and strain into a chilled cocktail glass. Like the Silver Bullet, the Silver Streak takes no garnish.

Singapore Sling

There are Slings and there are Slings, a preponderance of recipes so numerous that even our oldest and most trusted sources don't agree on a single formula. Some call for dry gin, some for sloe. Some call for citrus juices, some for none. Some insist on cherry brandy, some on apricot, some on both. The plentitude stems from the fact that slings were popular

> Singapore stands at the crossroads of the East, and whoever has been to Singapore knows Raffles. Just looking around the terrace porch, we've seen Frank Buck, the Sultan of Johore, Aimee Semple McPherson, Somerset Maugham, Dick Halliburton, Doug Fairbanks, Bob Ripley, Ruth Elder and Walter Camp— not that this is any wonder.

> ~Charles Baker, THE GENTLEMAN'S COMPANION, 1939

throughout the Pacific, and the worldwide drinking culture that flourished between the wars brought all these recipes home with them. The most famous, and certainly one of the earliest, slings was created in 1915 by Ngiam Tong Boon, barman at the famous Raffles Hotel, in Singapore. According to our favorite *bon vivant* of the era, Charles Baker, the Raffles Sling was "immortal…never forgotten…a delicious, slow-acting, insidious thing." We couldn't agree more. The recipe, now nearly a hundred years old, is still spectacular.

Singapore Sling

1 lime

1 oz. gin

1 oz. cherry brandy

1 oz. benedictine

Club soda

Begin by peeling the lime in a continuous spiral, taking care that no white fiber adheres to the peel. Set aside. Combine gin, cherry brandy, and benedictine in mixing glass with several ice cubes. Stir. (It is also permissible to combine in a shaker and shake.) Strain into a collins glass into which several ice cubes have been placed. Fill with club soda, add the entire lime peel, and serve with a swizzle stick.

VARIATION: Many Pacific watering holes used ginger ale in place of club soda, with equally delicious results.

FOR YOUR FURTHER DRINKING PLEASURE: Another popular drink of the era was the Straits Sling. To make this delightful and fruitier concoction, follow the recipe for the Raffles gin sling above, but add 2 tsp. lemon juice and 1 or 2 dashes each (depending on your taste) of Angostura and orange bitters.

MOONLIGHT COCKTAIL

Lyric by
KIM GANNON

Music by
LUCKY ROBERTS

PIANO SOLO ARRANGEMENT
NOW AVAILABLE

Introduced and Recorded by
GLENN MILLER
and his Orchestra

JEWEL MUSIC PUBLISHING CO., INC. • 1674 Broadway, New York, N. Y.

Sours

ssentially a Collins without the fizz, a Sour is one of America's oldest cocktails. The original, drunk when Scarlett O'Hara was still a toddler, was made with brandy and egg white. That version was abandoned as French imports became less common and Southerners learned to distill their own spirits. By the early 1900s, whiskey had replaced brandy as the spirit of choice for most Sour enthusiasts. During the 1920s and 30s, brandy reasserted itself in the form of the Pisco Sour, a cocktail made from Chilean pisco brandy, which was, at the time, readily available in the United States. Pisco is no longer a common bar finding, but if you sight a bottle, we heartily recommend it for consideration.

Whiskey Sour

$1\frac{1}{2}$ oz. rye or bourbon whiskey

Juice of $\frac{1}{2}$ lemon, strained of seeds

Juice of $\frac{1}{2}$ lime, strained of seeds

1 tsp. powdered sugar

Orange-slice garnish

Maraschino cherry garnish

Place whiskey, lemon and lime juices, and powdered sugar into a shaker with cracked ice. Shake vigorously. Strain into a chilled cocktail glass and add garnishes.

VARIATIONS: This recipe can be used to create several other sours, including:

BRANDY SOUR

GIN SOUR

PISCO SOUR

RUM SOUR

FOR YOUR FURTHER DRINKING PLEASURE: Two other, only slightly more complicated, Sours also deserve mention. The first is the Applejack Sour, made like a Whiskey Sour but with applejack and a generous dash of grenadine. Increase the amount of grenadine to a full ounce, and you have the delightfully crimsoned Fireman's Sour.

OLD CROW

Collection of GREAT BOURBON DRINK RECIPES

Stinger

Invented around 1900, the Stinger hit its peak of popularity during Prohibition, perhaps because the menthe overrode the taste of counterfeit booze. The Stinger has always been a love-it-or-hate-it cocktail, with writers Ian Fleming and Somerset Maugham firmly in the drink's favor. One of the best bits of Stinger lore is this anecdote: when garrulous British explorer Wilfred Thesiger heard of Evelyn Waugh's penchant for the drink, he observed that the preference was "just the sort of affectation" he expected of Waugh.

1¹/₂ oz. brandy

1¹/₂ oz. white crème de menthe

To make a classic Stinger, combine brandy and crème de menthe in a mixing glass with cracked ice. Mix, then strain into a chilled cocktail glass. An alternate, more modern, method is to fill an old-fashioned glass with ice, pour in the spirits, stir, and serve.

NOTE: Please do not do this fine old drink the disservice of making it with green crème de menthe.

Stone Fence

Order a Stone Fence these days, and you're likely to get a scotch and soda with a dash of bitters. But the original Stone Fence, dating from the early years of the twentieth century, was a true individual—one well worth bringing back.

2 oz. applejack

2 dashes Angostura bitters

Sweet apple cider

Place 2 or 3 ice cubes in an old-fashioned glass, add applejack and bitters, then fill with cold cider.

THE PRICE OF FUN IN THE 1920s:

Pack of gold-tipped cigarettes: 10¢

Metropolitan Opera matinee: $5 (orchestra seats)

Ladies silk stockings: $3

Around-the-world cruise: $1,000

THE PRICE OF FUN IN THE 1930s:

Fifth of whiskey: $3-4

Movie: 3¢

Dinner at a good New York restaurant: $1.50

Drink at Rockefeller Center: 25¢ (double)

Tequila Cocktail

Like many, we believed that the Tequila Sunrise was a thoroughly modern concoction—until we found this recipe. Called simply a "Tequila Cocktail," the formula dates from the 1930s and offers the same blend of orange, grenadine, and tequila as its boisterous grandchild—but far less flamboyantly and with a good deal more sophistication.

2 oz. tequila

1 dash grenadine

1 dash orange-flower water

Juice of 1 lime, strained of seeds

Place all ingredients into a blender with cracked ice or into a cocktail shaker with very finely crushed ice. Whir or shake sharply and quickly, then pour into a chilled oversize cocktail glass or an old-fashioned glass.

THE PRICE OF FUN IN THE 1940s:
Broadway show: $3-4
(evening, good seats)
Dinner and floor show at the
Copacabana $2.50
Fifth of whiskey: $4
Two dozen roses: $2

THE PRICE OF FUN IN THE 1950s:
Quart of gin: $3.50
Fifth of whiskey: $5
Large pizza: 75¢
Chinese dinner, with egg roll and
fortune cookie: $1.50

Zombie

Created in the mid-1930s, the Zombie became a nationally known celebrity when it was served at the Hurricane Bar at the New York World's Fair in 1939. Of the many "original" recipes, the most famous is credited to Don Beach of Hollywood's Don the Beachcomber. He first made the drink for a patron complaining of a hangover, no doubt working under the theory that the concoction would soon consign the hangover and much else to oblivion.

Why people drink them I don't know . . . Personally, I think it's too damn strong, but people seem to like it that way. ~Vic Bergeron (aka Trader Vic) on the Zombie, c. 1945

1 oz. white rum

1 oz. golden rum

1 oz. dark rum

1/2 oz. apple, apricot, or cherry brandy

3/4 oz. pineapple juice

3/4 oz. papaya juice

Juice of one lime, strained of seeds

151-proof rum

Pineapple-slice garnish

Combine all ingredients except 151-proof rum and garnishes in a shaker with cracked ice. Shake, then strain into a collins glass that has been filled with ice cubes or a good amount of crushed ice. Float a spoonful of 151 on top, then add garnishes, serve, and step back to avoid falling bodies.

Index

Acknowledgments

Photographs on pages 2, 9, 14, 26, 30, 52, 58, and 73 by permission CORBIS-Bettmann Archive.

A hearty toast to friends and colleagues who shared their vintage art with us:

Chisholm-Larsson Gallery
145 Eighth Avenue
New York, New York 10011
212-741-1703
http://www.chisholm-poster.com

Poster America
138 W. 18th St.
New York, New York 10011-5403
212-206-0499
http://www.posterfair.com

Fires Out Collectibles
Box 432
Boystown, Nebraska 68010-0432
402-496-1356

Thanks to Thomas Justino, our art researcher.

And a final tip of the hat to the traders at E-bay.com, who were prompt and professional without fail. Additional photo credits: SMP Graphics New York, NY.

Bibliography

96

In a world littered with bar guides, there are a few that are peerless. In preparing this book, we turned to them time and time again on matters of ingredients, method, history, and authenticity. Unfortunately, like all too many of the drinks they embrace, these drinkingman's bibles have fallen by the wayside and are, regretfully, out of print. But if you happen to run across one at a library, bookstore, or rummage sale, don't miss the opportunity to browse its pages.

Baker, Charles: *The Gentleman's Companion Vol. II: An Exotic Drinking Book, or Around the World with Jigger, Beaker and Flask*; Derrydale Press, 1939.

Baker, Charles: *The South American Gentleman's Companion: An Exotic Drinking Book, or Up and Down the Anders with Jigger, Beaker & Flask*; Crown, 1951.

Beebe, Lucious: *The Stork Club Bar Book*; Rinehart & Co., 1946.

Birmingham, Frederic, ed.: *Esquire Drink Book*; Raper & Row, 1956.

Craddock, Harry: *The Savoy Cocktail Book*; Richard Smith, 1930.

Duffy, Patrick Gavin: *The Official Mixer's Manual*; Alta Publications, 1934.

Thomas, "Professor" Jerry: *The Bon Vivant's Companion*; Alfred A. Knopf, 1927.

Whitfield, W.C.: *Here's How: Mixed Drinks;* Three Mountaineers, 1941.